Mariel Irvine, solicitor and principal of Mariel Irvine Solicitors, founded the firm in 2002, after some years as a partner in an insurance litigation firm in the City. She advised the police, insurers and the metal recycling industry on the drafting of the Scrap Metal Dealers Act 2013, and also its subsequent review by the Home Office in 2017. Scrap metal dealers come to her for advice on licensing, and also compliance with the General Data Protection Regulation and the Data Protection Act 2018.

Insurers, police, the Prison Governors' Association, the Police Superintendents' Association, the British Metal Recycling Association and others regularly instruct her regarding assault, stress at work and harassment claims; inquests and inquiries; pay, discrimination and other employment disputes; and privacy and data protection issues.

Chambers has recommended Mariel as a leading practitioner in Police Law over a number of years. In 2018 the Parliamentary Review, an independent publication which aims to share best practice among policy makers and business leaders, invited her to contribute to their inaugural Law and Justice Review, as a best practice representative. She regularly gives presentations and seminars.

A Practical Guide to the Scrap Metal Dealers Act 2013

A Practical Guide to the Scrap Metal Dealers Act 2013

Mariel Irvine

Law Brief Publishing

Published 2019 by Law Brief Publishing, an imprint of Law Brief Publishing Ltd
30 The Parks
Minehead
Somerset
TA24 8BT

www.lawbriefpublishing.com

Paperback: 978-1-911035-80-0

For Sam

PREFACE

The meaning of the Scrap Metal Dealers Act 2013 is broader than appears on an initial reading and possibly broader than was intended. There may be individuals and organisations trading in scrap metal who do not know they are caught by its provisions, although it provides a mandatory licensing regime for the metal recycling industry, bans trading in cash and creates new criminal offences that carry unlimited fines.

The absence of case law on the Act's meaning and effect may reflect widespread compliance. It may also reflect a low level of enforcement activity. In the absence of guidance from the courts, this book aims to place the Act in context and highlight its ambiguities and possibilities. It contains a chapter on data protection, as an extension of the Act's identity and record keeping requirements.

I would like to thank Tim Kevan and Garry Wright for their perseverance and encouragement.

The law is as stated on 17 October 2019.

Mariel Irvine
October 2019

CONTENTS

CHAPTER ONE
INTRODUCTION

Metal recycling is concerned with breaking down items that are past their useful life into their constituent metals. The industry is worth about £7 billion per annum, most of which comes from exports.

Those who carry out this work are generally known as scrap metal dealers or metal recyclers. They range from sole traders to multinational organisations. There are families who have been scrap metal dealers for generations. Some dealers trade from a yard. Others have no yard but collect scrap metal from door to door and transport it to the yards where they sell it. They are known as mobile collectors.

Once an item has been recycled it generally becomes unrecognisable. For example, catalytic converters may be recycled to extract palladium, radium and aluminium. Air conditioners may be recycled to extract copper from tubing. In the absence of records, it may be impossible to trace where any palladium, radium, aluminium or copper came from.

Three years ago, the general public began to focus its attention on metal recyclers. An increase in copper and other metal prices was triggering a corresponding increase in metal theft, and the dealers provided an easy way for thieves to translate stolen items into cash. They became more daring as the value of metal rose. They stole sculptures, lead tiles from church rooves and metal plaques from war memorials. The emotional fallout from these thefts attracted media interest, as did the practical effect which was often much greater than the value of the metal stolen. Copper cabling taken from the railway and worth £20 could cause many hours of train delay and cost the railway infrastructure and train operating companies thousands of pounds in fines and compensation. Moreover, travelling members of the public were being delayed, inconvenienced and stressed.

Various organisations began to lobby for legislative change and the problem began to attract the attention of politicians. A ban on cash trading was proposed and introduced as a stop gap measure. The ultimate solution was the Scrap Metal Dealers Act 2013 (the Act), which came into effect on 1 October 2013. It affirmed the ban on cash, created a licensing regime for dealers, and introduced record keeping and identity checking requirements, alongside new criminal offences.

In 2017, the mandatory five-year review of the effectiveness of the Act confirmed that metal thefts recorded by the police in England and Wales had fallen from 62,000 per year in 2012 to 2013, to fewer than 13,000 in 2016 to 2017. Minister for Crime, Safeguarding and Vulnerability, Victoria Atkins, said:

> *Metal thefts can have a hugely negative impact on victims and the wider community, particularly when items which form part of our nation's heritage such as war memorials, the statues in our parks and town centres, or other sites of religious, community or cultural value are callously targeted.*

> *I am pleased the Act continues to be a powerful weapon against this form of criminality and the robust measures put in place in 2013 are working to regulate the industry and deter people from stealing metal or dealing with stolen scrap metal.*

However, insurers, trade associations and others fear that metal thefts continue, particularly when the value of copper and other metal rises. Insurers are requiring churches to install CCTV cameras as a condition of insurance on account of the continuing risk. Local media outlets across the country report significant increases in metal theft over the past two years. There is a sense that more could be done to enforce the Act and the absence of reported cases on the Act's meaning and effect may confirm this.

This book reviews the Scrap Metal Dealers Act 2013, and covers:-

- Scrap Metal Dealers' Act 1964 and interim measures (Chapter 2)

- Scrap Metal Dealers Act 2013 and Home Office Guidance (Chapter 3)

- Meaning of scrap metal dealer, mobile collector and motor salvage operator (Chapter 4)

- Licensing regime: determining suitability and terms of licence (Chapter 5)

- Licensing regime: procedure (Chapter 6)

- Ban on cash (Chapter 7)

- Identification and recording requirements (Chapter 8)

- Data protection (Chapter 9)

- Powers of enforcement (Chapter 10)

- Criminal offences (Chapter 11)

CHAPTER TWO
SCRAP METAL DEALERS ACT 1964
AND INTERIM MEASURES

Until the Act came into force on 1 October 2013, the scrap metal industry had been ineffectually "governed" by an act that was almost 50 years old: the Scrap Metal Dealers Act 1964. Its provisions had largely fallen into disuse. Although section 1 imposed a requirement on local authorities to maintain a register of scrap metal dealers, and prohibited unregistered scrap metal dealers from trading, a number of large and reputable organisations ignored, or were ignorant of, this requirement. Section 1(9) imposed a duty on every local authority to enforce the registration requirement but the local authorities tended not to do so, even though breach of the registration provision was a criminal offence punishable by a fine. Moreover, although it was an offence to trade without registering, the requirement had little regulatory function since registration was automatic upon receipt of an application that provided the specified particulars. The 2013 Act gives local authorities a regulatory function by creating a licensing regime, reviewed in more detail at Chapters 5 and 6.

The 1964 Act set out record-keeping requirements. Every dealer was to keep a book in which particulars were recorded of all scrap metal "received" and "all scrap metal either processed at or despatched from that place". Under section 2 (2) the information to be recorded included the description and weight of the metal received, the date and time of receipt, the name and address of the person from whom it was received, the registration number of any vehicle used to deliver metal and any price paid for the metal. The same information *mutatis mutandis* was to be recorded in relation to scrap metal processed or dispatched, except no vehicle registration number plate was required. Separate books could be kept for metal received, and for metal processed or dispatched. However, not more than one book could be kept for each category at a given time.

The price paid or received for metal was to be recorded, or the estimated value of the metal immediately before the transaction in those deals where the price had not yet been fixed or where no price was to be paid. Section 2 envisaged payment in kind ie whole or part exchange. It also envisaged the possibility that some metal might be received or dispatched for free, without any sort of payment. Failure to comply with recording requirements was a strict liability offence punishable by a fine.

The standards of record keeping were generally poor. It was often very difficult to identify scrap metal received from the vague descriptions entered in the book. After it had been macerated it was impossible to establish what scrap metal had been taken into the yard. The recorded particulars of the name and address were often incomplete. There was no requirement to check the supplier's identity. The new Act stipulates that a more detailed description of the metal is to be provided and the suppliers' identity verified. These new requirements are covered in more detail in Chapter 8.

There were special provisions for itinerant (now known as mobile) collectors. After consulting with the police, a local authority could make an order exempting them from the more formal record-keeping requirements set out above and subjecting them to a less rigorous regime, limited to recording the weight of items sold and the sale price. The 2013 Act makes a more limited distinction between mobile collectors and other dealers. Both are subject to the same recording regime when receiving scrap metal. When disposing of it, mobile collectors need not record any description of the metal or the price or other payment received. They must simply record the date and time of disposal and full name and address of the person to whom the metal was transferred.

Under the old regime, it was envisaged that itinerant collectors could have scrap metal stores while they received and disposed of metal in transactions elsewhere. Under the new regime any use of a fixed site or scrap metal store takes a dealer outside the definition of mobile collector.

The 1964 Act gave magistrates the power to impose additional requirements on dealers who were convicted of any offence of dishonesty, or of trading without first registering with the local authority, or of failing to comply with the recording requirements described above. These additional requirements were: (1) that no scrap metal could be received at a scrap metal store between the hours of 6 o'clock in the evening and 8 o'clock in the morning and (2) all scrap metal received at such a store to be kept, in the form in which it was received there, for a period of not less than 72 hours beginning with the time when it was received. Any such order could be specified to remain in force for a period of up to 2 years. These conditions are replicated in the new Act, with some minor modifications.

Under section 5 it was an offence to acquire any scrap metal from a person "apparently" under the age of 16 years. There is no similar offence in the new Act.

The police were concerned that they had no power under the old Act to enter premises that were not registered. Constables had a right of entry and inspection to all places that were registered as a scrap metal store and to require the production of, and to inspect any scrap metal kept at that place and any book the dealer was required to keep. An officer of the local authority, duly authorised in writing by the authority, had the power to enter any premises he had reasonable grounds for believing was being used as a scrap metal store and was not registered as such. It did not make sense that the police did not have the same power of entry into unregistered premises.

A justice of the peace could authorise the constable or officer of the local authority to enter a scrap metal store by force. Under the new Act, a justice of the peace may issue a warrant allowing police to enter unlicensed premises where there are *reasonable grounds for believing that the premises are being used by a scrap metal dealer in the course of business.* (see section 16 (6)). It also provides a system for closure orders which are considered in Chapter 10.

When metal theft became a high-profile issue, Parliament made amendments to the 1964 Act as a stop gap measure, before the introduction of the 2013 Act. These amendments came into effect on 3 December 2012, via section 146 of the Legal Aid, Sentencing and Punishment of Offenders Act 2012 (LASPO), and were designed to facilitate the tracing of stolen metal and also money laundering. They are largely replicated in the Scrap Metal Dealers Act 2013.

The amendments were:-

- a ban on cash trading

- police right of entry into scrap metal stores where there were reasonable grounds for believing that payments continued to be made in cash

- increase in financial penalties for criminal offences under the 1964 Act.

CHAPTER THREE
SCRAP METAL DEALERS ACT 2013
AND HOME OFFICE GUIDANCE

On an initial reading the Scrap Metal Dealers Act 2013 seems to be a clever, neat and effective solution to the problem of metal theft. It provides a licensing regime to regulate the industry, replicates the ban on cash contained in LASPO, imposes identification requirements for suppliers, gives justices of the peace powers to issue warrants authorising both police and local authority officers to enter licensed and unlicensed premises by force if necessary, and introduces a system of closure orders for unlicensed sites.

However, on closer scrutiny the meaning of ordinary words and phrases becomes elusive or ambiguous, particularly when applied to real life situations. For example, what does "partly" mean when considering whether a person is a scrap metal dealer? 1n deciding whether a license should be issued, the local authority must assess whether the applicant is "suitable". What does this mean? How are dealers to record a "description" of scrap metal received? For example, is it sufficient to call a lorry load of railway line, "iron lengths"?

The reality is that the meaning and implications of various salient features of the Act are likely to require clarification by the courts. However, there has been no reported clarification in the six years since the Act was implemented.

The Home Office attempted to provide clarification by giving guidance on provisions of particular concern to the metal recycling industry and other affected parties. On others, it has given draft guidance only to change that guidance or omit it on publication. In one instance it published guidance, only to reverse it subsequently and then change it back to the original version.

When the Act came into force on 1 October 2013, the Home Office issued "Supplementary Guidance on the Scrap Metal Dealers Act 2013". It was updated in December 2013. However, the guidance is not the law, which is contained in the Act. The guidance may be persuasive and the courts are likely to take it into account when deciding what a given statutory provision means. Enforcement authorities may use the guidance as a basis for decision making, and convicted defendants might rely on it in mitigation. However, the courts may ignore it as they think fit.

The breadth of the new Act and the confusion surrounding it is usefully illustrated by the manufacturing exemption at section 21 (3). Manufacturers who *sell* scrap metal *"only as a by product of manufacturing articles or as surplus materials not required for manufacturing them"* are not carrying on business as scrap metal dealers.

The Scrap Metal Dealers Act 1964 created an exemption for manufacturers who *buy* scrap metal for their manufacturing processes, as well as sell it on afterwards. Against this background it is assumed that Parliament intended to limit the ambit of this exclusion in the new Act. However, the Home Office does not agree. In the face of protest from metal manufacturers who buy scrap metal, such as those who make stainless steel, the Home Office updated its Supplementary Guidance of October 2013 with the insertion of a new paragraph 2.6. It provides:

> *"Producers of ferrous and non- ferrous metals purchase processed scrap metal as a raw material used in their manufacturing process. Whilst on a case by case basis this may meet the test of wholly or partly buying or selling scrap metal, the Act was never intended to*

extend beyond those who were expected to register under the Scrap Metal Dealers Act 1964 or the Vehicles (Crime) Act 2001 which this Act replaces. Therefore, we do not intend these companies to be required to comply with the licensing requirement. We have communicated this to appropriate industry associations via the Department for Business, Innovation and Skills."

Many metal manufacturers took legal advice and applied for licenses, notwithstanding the Home Office guidance.

CHAPTER FOUR
MEANING OF SCRAP METAL DEALER, MOBILE COLLECTOR AND MOTOR SALVAGE OPERATOR

Who is a scrap metal dealer?

There is more than one question to be answered when considering the definition. The first step is to consider what "scrap metal" is. Section 21(6) of the Act defines it as including:

> "(a) any old, waste or discarded metal or metallic material, and
>
> (b) any product, article or assembly which is made from or contains metal and is broken, won out or regarded by its last holder as having reached the end of its useful life."

This appears to be a satisfactory and self-evident description encompassing what scrap metal is and those items past their useful life that may contain scrap metal. However, it is not an exclusive definition. It is an inclusive one. The parliamentary draftsmen wanted to retain room for manoeuvre. An item may fall outside the strict definition and still fall within the meaning of scrap metal for the purposes of the Act. Perhaps in some circumstances second hand goods might be caught.

Under section 22 (7) neither gold, silver nor any alloy with more than 2% of its weight attributable to gold or silver, falls within the definition.

If a person is likely to be handling scrap metal, the next step is to consider what "carrying on business as a scrap metal dealer" means. Section 21 (2):

> "*A person carries on business as a scrap metal dealer if the person-*
>
> (a) *carries on a business which consists wholly or **partly in buying or selling** scrap metal, whether or not the metal is sold in the form in which it was bought, or*
>
> (b) *carries on business as a motor salvage operator (so far as that does not fall within paragraph (a)*" [Emphasis added]

The definition of person within a statute covers a company or other legal entity unless the contrary is provided. A scrap metal dealer can be a limited company, a partnership, an unincorporated association or a sole trader.

Who is a motor salvage operator?

It is important to note that motor vehicle salvage operators fall within the ambit of the new Act, which repeals Part 1 of the Vehicles (Crime) Act 2001 and the Motor Salvage Operators Regulations 2002. This superceded legislation provided a formal system of registration with the local authority.

Section 21 (4) provides:-

> "*For the purposes of subsection (2)(b), a person carries on business as a motor salvage operator if the person carries on a business which consists –*

(a) *wholly or partly in recovering salvageable parts from motor vehicles for re-use or sale and subsequently selling or otherwise disposing of the rest of the vehicle for scrap,*

(b) *wholly or mainly in buying written-off vehicles and subsequently repairing and reselling them,*

(c) *wholly or mainly in buying or selling motor vehicles which are to be the subject (whether immediately or on a subsequent resale) of any of the activities mentioned in paragraphs (a) and (b), or*

(d) *wholly or mainly in activities falling within paragraphs (b) and (c).*

When the Act was introduced there was some concern that motor salvage operators might argue they were trading in second hand cars to avoid the ban on buying scrap metal for cash. The Home Office guidance (see above) explains:-

Issuing a certificate of destruction would clearly indicate that a vehicle is scrap and a trader should not in those circumstances pay cash for it. Where a certificate is not issued, factors such as whether the car has a valid MOT and is drivable without repair, and also whether the dealer has facilities for repairing vehicles and a history of selling vehicles, will indicate if it is second hand or scrap.

Responders to the Home Office review of the effectiveness of the Act suggested that the legal definition of scrap metal be extended to include any business involved in buying secondhand vehicles.

What does *partly* mean?

There is no definition of what *partly* means. It is clear that it does not mean mainly as this word is also used in ihe definition for carrying out a business as a motor salvage operator under section 21.

The Home Office originally gave an informal indication that the income generated from the sale of scrap metal would need to be *"a key component of the total income"* in order to come within the meaning of "partly" and satisfy the test for carrying on a business as a scrap metal dealer under section 21 (2) (a) . A distinction was drawn between "partly" or a "key component", and "incidental". Where the buying and selling of scrap metal was only an "incidental" aspect of the business, it might not fall within the ambit of the Act.

In its published supplementary guidance of October 2013, the Home Office abandoned its use of the word "incidental". At paragraph 2.3 it simply concedes that it will be a question of fact for the court to decide whether the buying or selling of scrap metal forms such a "minimal" part of a person's business that it does not fall within the Act. It notes that: *there are many factors a court may consider in reaching its judgement such as the proportion of the business related to scrap metal in terms of value or volume.*

Despite this submission to the will of the courts, the Home Office proceeds to express its views on whether skip hire companies, tradespersons and civic amenity sites are carrying on business as scrap metal dealers. At paragraph 2.8 the advice in relation to skip hire companies is fairly tentative: ... *a company that only rents skips to households where recoverable scrap metal forms a minor part of the skip contents and the company's business may not require a license.* Again, it will be a question of fact for the courts to decide.

The advice on tradespersons is more categorical at paragraph 2.9: *Tradespersons will not require a scrap metal dealers license if buying or selling scrap metal is an incidental function of their business (eg being a plumber or electrician.).* The word "incidental" crops up again without any foundation in the wording of the Act.

The guidance at paragraph 2.11 of the supplementary guidance on civic amenity sites is clear cut: *Civic amenity sites, run by councils or contracted out to others, will not require a license.* Why not? The 1964 Act accepted that local authorities might carry out business as scrap metal dealers in which event they needed to be registered as such, although they were exempt from the formal application requirements. The 2013 Act makes no provision for local authorities and in the absence of such an exclusion they are arguably caught within the same regime as others who deal in scrap metal.

The Local Government Association agrees with the Home Office. It argues that councils have a statutory duty to collect household waste and any resulting sales are incidental to this obligation. Furthermore, in 2013 only about 7.3 % of material recycled by councils is metal so it is only a small proportion and the income from it is insignificant.

When determining whether a person carries on business as a scrap metal dealer and requires a license, local authorities have been advised to consider whether the buying or selling of scrap metal forms an *integral* part of the business. Is it sold as a by-product from a manufacturing process? Is the buying and selling of scrap metal advertised?

Arguably anyone who recovers any salvageable parts from a motor vehicle for re-use before disposing of the vehicle under section 21 (4) (a) may be fall within the definition of a vehicle salvage operator and require a scrap metal dealers license.

The phrase *scrap metal dealer* is likely to be a fluid and flexible concept within the meaning of the Act. By the Home Office's own admission, it appears to mean more than was intended. The extent of its meaning is to be determined by the courts on a case by case basis.

Who is a mobile collector?

Under section 22 (4) "*Mobile collector means a person who*

(a) *Carries on business as a scrap metal dealer otherwise than at a site, and*

(b) *Regularly engages, in the courses of that business, in collecting waste materials and old, broken, worn out or defenced articles by means of visits from door to door.*"

Visits from door to door may refer to speculative visits, rather than pre-arranged appointments. Section 2.12 of the Home Office supplementary guidance updated in December 2013 provides:-

If a scrap metal dealer (who is a motor salvage operator) holds a site license and employs or sub-contracts a company to pick up cars on the company's behalf in the course of the business from that site we do not consider that they will need individual mobile collectors licenses as this is not regularly engaging in collection of waste materials and old, broken, worn out or defaced articles by means of visits from door to door but pre-arranged appointments.

CHAPTER FIVE
LICENSING REGIME – DETERMINING SUITABILITY AND TERMS OF LICENCE

It has been unlawful for scrap metal dealers (including mobile collectors and vehicle salvage operators) to carry on business without a licence since the Act came into force on 1 October 2013. It has been a criminal offence to trade without a license since 1 December 2013. A license is valid for three years and must be renewed before it expires.

The licensing regime is administered by local authorities and enforced by both local authorities and the police.

Types of licenses and their display

There are two types of license, a site license and a collector's license, depending on whether the scrap metal dealer is a mobile collector or not.

A site license covers all the sites or yards within the boundaries of the local authority issuing the license. The sites are identified on the license, together with the name of the site manager responsible for each. Under section 22 (9) a site *means any premises used in the course of carrying on business as a scrap metal dealer (whether or not metal is kept there).* According to the Local Government Guide to the Scrap Metal Dealers Act 2013, published shortly before it came into force, this means a site licence is needed for an office, even if the dealer does not operate a scrap metal store or yard. This begs the question whether mobile collectors who have offices at home are scrap metal dealers. It is clear that a scrap metal dealer cannot hold both a site and mobile collector's licence from the same council (see section 2 (9)).

A collector's license covers scrap metal dealing (whether buying or selling) within the boundaries of the local authority issuing the license. More than one license may be required where a mobile collector buys or sells scrap across different local authority boundaries, or a dealer has sites or yards in more than one local authority area.

Under section 2 (8) the Secretary of State may prescribe further requirements as to the form and content of licenses. No further regulations have been put in place as yet.

Licenses must be issued in a form that allows them to be displayed. Section 10 requires a scrap metal dealer who holds a site license *to display it at each site identified in the license… in a prominent place in an area accessible to the public.* A collector's license must be displayed *in any vehicle that is being used in the course of the dealer's business … in a manner which enables it easily to be read by a person outside the vehicle.*

Failure to display the license is a criminal offence.

Who is a suitable person to be a scrap metal dealer?

Under section 3 (1) a local authority must be satisfied that the applicant is a *suitable person* (rather than the *fit and proper person* under the Vehicles (Crime) Act 2001) to carry on business as a scrap metal dealer before issuing a license.

Under section 3 (2), in making such a determination the local authority *"may have regard to any information which it considers to be relevant including in particular* :-

(a) *whether the applicant or any site manager has been convicted of a relevant offence;*

(b) *whether either has been subject to any relevant enforcement action;*

(c) *any previous refusal of an application for the issue or renewal of a scrap metal license (and the reasons for the refusal):*

(d) *any previous refusal of an application for a relevant environmental permit or registration (and the reasons for this)*

(e) *any previous revocation of a scrap metal license (and the reasons for the revocation)*

(f) *whether the applicant has demonstrated that there will be in place adequate procedures to ensure the provisions of this Act will be complied with.*

There is no requirement that the local authority take into account any of the factors listed in section 3 (2) (including whether a site manager has been convicted of a relevant offence). Furthermore, there is no restriction on the factors that a local authority may take into account when assessing suitability. Under paragraph 4(1) of Schedule 1 of the Act, *the local authority may request (either when the application is made or later) that the applicant provide such further information as the authority considers relevant for the purpose of considering the application.* If the information is not provided the authority may *decline to proceed with the application* under paragraph 4 (2).

There are fears within the scrap metal industry that unrelated issues, such as planning applications and political concerns, may unfairly influence decisions. However, authorities may legitimately take into account any unlawful behaviour, such as the fact that a scrap metal yard has been operating for some time without the requisite planning permission, or that the organisation is not registered with the Information Commissioner under the Data Protection Act 2018 (see Chapter 9). (Many scrap metal dealers have CCTV cameras that record transactions on site. This information is likely to fall within the definition of personal data under the General Data Protection Regulation and Data Protection Act 2018 (DPA). The ICO has issued a code of practice that provides recommendations on the use of CCTV systems to help organisations comply with the DPA.) Such behaviour on its own is unlikely to be sufficient to support a decision that the dealer is unsuitable for a licence, assuming steps are taken to rectify it.

In assessing suitability, the local authority must not only consider whether the applicant and any proposed site managers have been convicted of relevant offences and/or subjected to relevant enforcement action. Where the applicant is a company, the authority must consider the suitability of any director, secretary or shadow director of the company. Where the applicant is a partnership, it must consider the suitability of each of the partners. (See section 3 (4) and (5) of the Act.)

Under section 3 (2) (a) a site manager refers to the persons proposed in the application to fulfil this role. Section 22 (10) defines a *site manager* as *the individual who exercises day-to-day control and management of activities at the site.* Under subsection 11 an individual may be named as site manager at more than one site but no site may have more than one site manager.

When considering whether there are adequate procedures in place to ensure compliance with the Act under section 3 (2) (f), the guidance highlights these requirements:

- procedures for verifying the supplier's identity under section 11;

- procedures for paying for scrap metal by means other than cash (section 12 creates an offence of paying cash for scrap metal);

- procedures for keeping records under section 15;

The authority might also consider what security arrangements are in place to prevent the unlawful purchase, sale or theft of scrap metal. Mobile collectors may be asked for details of the vehicles they are using and where they are stored when not in use. Where there are concerns that the applicant may be using cash, the local authority may wish to check the bank account details.

When a licence is refused full reasons should be given for the decision.

Paragraph 3.7 of Home Office statutory guidance to local authorities when determining suitability (see below) provides: *Tacit consent should not apply in relation to scrap metal dealer licence applications as there is an overriding public interest in ensuring that the suitability of applicants is assessed before the licence is issued.*

However, concerns remain that the suitability test is not being rigorously applied.

What are relevant offences?

The *Scrap Metal Dealers Act 2013 (Prescribed Relevant Offences and Relevant Enforcement Action) Regulations 2013* are in line with the criteria used by the Environment Agency when issuing environmental permits under the Environmental Protection Act 1990. The regulations provide a schedule of relevant offences for the purposes of section 3(3)(b) and (c). They include various environment related offences and also any offence under:

- the Waste (Electrical and Electronic Equipment) Regulations 2006

- section 1 Fraud Act 2006 where the offence relates to scrap metal or the environment

- various sections of the Theft Act 1968 where the offence relates to scrap metal or the environment

- the Scrap Metal Dealers Acts 1964 and 2013;

- Part 1 of the Vehicles (Crime) Act 2001;

- section 146 Legal Aid, Sentencing and Punishment of Offenders Act 2012;

- sections 327, 328 or 330 to 332 Proceeds of Crime Act 2002

The offences extend to

- attempting or conspiring to commit any offences in the Schedule;

- inciting, aiding, abetting, counselling or procuring the commission of any of the offences within the Schedule;

- an offence under Part 2 Serious Crime Act 2007 (encouraging or assisting crime) committed in relation to any offence falling within the Schedule.

The Basic Disclosure Certificate (see Chapter 6 below), do not include spent convictions for relevant offences secured by the Environment Agency and/or Natural Resources Wales or other local authorities.

What is relevant enforcement action?

Under regulation 3, a person is subject to *relevant enforcement action* for the purposes of section 3 (3) (c) of the Act where

(a) *the person has been charged with an offence specified in the Schedule to these Regulations, and criminal proceedings in respect of that offence have not yet been concluded; or*

(b) *an environmental permit granted in respect of the person under the Environmental Permitting (England and Wales) Regulations 2010 has been revoked in whole, or partially revoked, to the extent that the permit no longer authorises the recovery of metal.*

Statutory guidance on determining suitability

The *authority must also have regard to any guidance on determining suitability which is issued from time to time by the Secretary of State* under section 3 *(6)*. The Secretary of State has issued guidance which was last revised in May 2014.

This guidance is addressed to local authorities and is clear that *a conviction for a relevant offence should not automatically lead to the refusal of a scrap metal dealer's licence. You may consult your local police force (section 3 (7) for further details about the offence including both the seriousness of the offence and the date when it was committed. Once you have this, you should consider it alongside any other information you may have regard to when determining suitability. If a site manager has been convicted of a relevant offence, the same process applies.*

Similarly, the guidance confirms that relevant enforcement action, such as a pending prosecution for a relevant offence, is not a sufficient basis for refusing a licence. The situation should be monitored and reviewed when there is an outcome. Where the applicant has been convicted of a relevant offence, consideration should be given to the impact this has on suitability and any necessary action taken such as the imposition of conditions or the revocation of the licence (see below).

Where the relevant enforcement action concerns the revocation of an environmental permit to the extent that it no longer authorises the recovery of metal, the authority should *consult with the Environment Agency and Natural Resources Wales* [section 3 (7)] *to find out the reasons for whole or partial revocation and consider if the reasons impact on their suitability.*

Some police forces have adopted a policy of objecting to the grant of a license to anybody who has a relevant offence. In 2011 there were many raids on scrap metal yards and a number of dealers were convicted of failing to keep records in contravention of the 1964 Act. It was a strict liability offence. Some of the offences were little more than administrative oversights, such as failing to include a house number for the supplier or omitting some part of the date when the metal was received. These errors were frequently made by the employee rather than the dealer applying for the license, in which case the new Act provides the dealer with a defence (see Chapter 10). The police may be willing to withdraw their objection once they appreciate the circumstances surrounding the offence. Once the objection is withdrawn the way may be clear for the local authority to grant the license.

More generally, if the police object to the granting of a licence on the grounds the person is unsuitable, it is clearly advisable the authority consult with other individuals and organisations, although this is not set out in the statutory guidance. The guidance is clear the local authority must make up its own mind as to whether a person is suitable.

The guidance covers spent convictions which should not be taken into account, except where *the local authority is satisfied that justice cannot be done except by admitting or requiring evidence relating to a person's spent convictions. In doing so, the local authority must have regard to the age, circumstances, relevance and seriousness of spent convictions*

Where an authority discovers that the applicant has a relevant conviction that was not disclosed on its application form, the guidance advises that the authority request further information from the application. The authority should consider whether the omission was deliberate and impacts on the applications suitability. Making a false statement in an application is a criminal offence and the authority may refer this to the police.

Information regarding scrap metal licenses

Local authorities must supply information relating to a scrap metal license or an application for a license when requested to do so by another local authority, the Environment Agency or the Natural Resources Body for Wales, or the police under section 6 of the Act.

Under section 7, the Environment Agency and the Natural Resources Body for Wales are both required to keep a public register of scrap metal licenses issued by local authorities. The information includes the expiry date of the license. Both agencies rely on local authorities to provide them with this information, which is not obligatory. The information contained on the register may be incomplete.

Previous refusal of application for scrap metal dealer's licence or environmental permit, or previous revocation of scrap metal dealer's licence.

The guidance advises the local authority to check its records to find out whether the applicant has been refused any previous applications for scrap metal dealer's licenses or environmental permits. The reasons for any refusal are to be considered and the authority is reminded of its ability to consult with other persons on the applicant's suitability, including the police and other local authorities.

The reasons for revoking a licence may not always impact on suitability. The guidance gives this example from section 4 (2) of the Act: a licence may be revoked where the site manager named on the licence does not act as site manager at any of the sites identified. This does not necessary mean that a later application for a licence should be refused.

Local authorities are also advised to check the register of scrap metal dealers held by the Environment Agency/Natural Resources Wales to find out whether an applicant's licence in any other local authority area has been revoked. Where a license has been revoked, the authority is advised to contact the relevant local authority for the reasons behind the revocation. Do these reasons still apply?

The statutory guidance advises: *It will be undesirable for a person who has been refused a licence by one local authority area to be issued a licence by another, therefore if a person has been refused a licence in a different local authority area, it will be important to scrutinise the reasons for refusal.* If, for example, the reason for refusal was that the applicant had failed to demonstrate that there were adequate procedures in place to ensure compliance with the Act, and those measures had since been put in place, then the reason for the revocation no longer applies.

It is suggested that local authorities routinely check whether an applicant is on the Environment Agency's or Natural Resources Wales register of permits and registrations: *if the applicant does not appear on the register and does not therefore hold a relevant environmental permit, exemption or registration then you may also wish to consult the Environment Agency or Natural Resources Wales as the applicant should not be operating as a scrap metal dealer without one or other of those.*

Consultation

The authority may, but is not obliged to, consult other persons on suitability such as other local authorities, the Environment Agency, the Natural Resources Body for Wales, and the police. The optional nature of this provision is curious, although in practice local authorities consult with others, particularly the police. The Local Government Association guidance recommends that the Environment Agency and the National Resources Wales public registers are checked for enforcement action. These organisations might also be contacted regarding any ongoing enforcement action.

For some time local authorities have been encouraged to notify their local police force of successful prosecutions for recordable offences under the Scrap Metal Dealers Act 2013. Compliance with this recommendation is probably not universal.

Conditions of licence

Instead of revoking a licence or refusing an application there is a half-way house that ensures the applicant can continue to trade although convicted of a relevant offence. Section 3 (8) provides:

If the applicant or any site manager has been convicted of a relevant offence, the authority may include in the license one or both of the following conditions –

(a) *that the dealer must not receive scrap metal except between 9 am and 5 pm on any day;*

(b) *that all scrap metal received must be kept in the form in which it is received for a specified period not exceeding 72 hours, beginning with the time when it is received.*

This section is obviously designed to allow monitoring and traceability by the police and local authority.

When the Act came into force there were authorities that drew up draft contracts for signature by the scrap metal dealers as a "condition" of issuing the license. Some contracts contained a long list of requirements, such as the installation of CCTV equipment. As it happens, a CCTV requirement was considered and rejected during the drafting of the Act, which does not delegate any condition making power to local authorities. The only conditions that may be imposed relating to the grant of a license are set out in section 3 (8) below.

Application to vary

An application may be made to vary a licence from one type to another (site licence to collector's licence and vice versa). The licensee *must* make an application when there is a change in the name of the licensee, the sites or the site manager. Failure to do so is a criminal offence.

Notification requirements

An applicant for a scrap metal licence or the renewal or variation a licence must notify the authority of any changes that materially affect the accuracy of the information provided in his application. Various other notification requirements are set out in section 8. Failure to comply with these requirements is a criminal offence.

CHAPTER SIX
LICENSING REGIME –
PROCEDURE

Licensing application

Paragraph 2 of Schedule 1 to the Act sets out the information which must be provided with a licensing application.

The mandatory information includes the full name, date of birth and usual place of residence of any individual applicant. Corporate applicants must provide the name and registration number of the company, together with the address of the company's registered office. Where an application is made by a partnership, the full name, date of birth and usual place of residence of each partner must be provided. Some authorities require these details for each of the directors of an applicant company, together with their photographs, although this is not mandatory requirement.

Details of any conviction of the applicant for a relevant offence, or any relevant enforcement action taken against the applicant, must be given. If the application is made by a company, this information is likely to be required of each of the directors, even though the statutory requirement is likely to be restricted to corporate offences and enforcement action. As explained above, a local authority may take into account any information which it considers to be relevant when assessing suitability. Where the applicant is a partnership ,the requirement is likely to extend to relevant offences committed by each of the partners.

The Home Office guide stipulates that local authorities must ask applicants to submit a Basic Disclosure Certificate for themselves, any person listed on the application form including any site manager, each partner if a partnership and, if a company, for the directors, shadow director and company secretary. The certificates are used to verify the information submitted in the application and to identify any relevant offences (see above).

The address of any site in the local authority area where the applicant carries on business as a scrap metal dealer or proposes to do so must also be included. If the application is successful, these addresses will be set out on the face of the license that is publicly displayed.

The full name, date of birth, and usual place of residence of each individual proposed to be named in the license as a site manager other than the applicant must be given. Details of any conviction or any enforcement action taken against the proposed site manager (s) must also be provided.

Additional information includes details of any relevant environmental permit or registration in relation to the applicant together with details of any other scrap metal license issued by that local authority or others within the three years ending with the date of the application.

Most importantly details of the bank account which is proposed to be used in order to comply with the ban on cash (see below) must also be provided.

Applications for a license maybe made online.

Licence fee

An application for a licence must be accompanied by the licence fee under Schedule 1 (6) of the 2013 Act. Under Schedule 1 (6) (2) … *The authority must have regard to any guidance issued from time to time by the Secretary of State with the approval of the Treasury* in setting a licence fee. On 12th of August 2013 the Home Office provided guidance on licence fee charges which states that it is binding on all authorities to the extent provided in Schedule 1 (6).

Local authorities may recover the costs stemming from administering and seeking compliance with the regime. Fees should be set with reference to the actual costs to each authority. In other words, the authority should ensure that the income from license fees does not exceed the cost of administering the licensing regime. The fee cannot be used to support enforcement activity against unlicensed scrap metal dealers, such as issuing closure notices and applying to the Magistrates Court for a warrant (see further below). Fees charged for site licences should reflect extra work involved in processing these applications and will vary from the fees charged for collectors' licences.

There remains a significant divergence in the licensing fees charged by local authorities. Respondents to the Home Office review of the effectiveness of the Act highlighted this divergence. When the Act was introduced, the lowest fees were under £100 and the highest over £2,000. The lowest fees did not appear to factor in any enforcement activity against those who were licensed. Enforcement activity against unlicensed dealers by way of closure orders or otherwise may not be included in the fee (see *Hemming v Westminster City Council* [2013] EWCA Civ 591). Such expenses must be met by the Authority's central funds.

Term of licence

The term of a license is three years beginning on the day when it was issued. After that period, it expires. Any application to renew a licence before it expires continues the licence term. If an application for a licence is refused, the licence expires when no appeal against the refusal is possible or when any appeal is finally determined or withdrawn (see paragraph 1 of Schedule 1.

Outcome of application for a licence

If a local authority proposes to refuse an application, or revoke or vary a licence under section 4, it must inform the applicant what it proposes to do and provide the reasons for it. It must allow not less than 14 days for the licensee to make representations or inform the authority that it wishes to do so. If the applicant fails to take either of these steps within the stipulated period, the authority may revoke or vary the licence as it proposes. If the licensee has notified the authority that it wishes to make representations, the authority must allow him a further reasonable period to do so.

If the licensee makes the representations within the stipulated period the authority must consider them. If the licensee informs the authority that it wishes to make oral representations the authority must give it the opportunity of appearing before it and being heard by a person appointed by the authority.

If the authority refuses the application or revokes or varies the licence it must give the licensee a notice setting out its decision with reasons. It must set out the time limit for appeal and, if it is a revocation or variation of the licence, the time when it takes effect.

There is a right of appeal to the Magistrates Court against:-

- the refusal of an application for a licence

- the inclusion of a condition in the licence under section 3 (8)

- the revocation or variation of a licence under section 4.

The appeal must be made within 21 days beginning on the day when notice was given. The procedure is by way of complaint for an order in accordance with sections 51 to 57 of the Magistrates Court Act 1980.

The Magistrates Court may confirm, vary or reverse the authority's decision and give such directions as it considers appropriate having regard to the provisions of the Act. The authority must comply with any directions given by the magistrates when the time for it making an application under section 111 MCA 1980 by way of case stated has passed

Revocation of a scrap metal dealers' licence

The authority may revoke a licence at any time if it is no longer satisfied that the licensee is a suitable person to carry on business as a scrap metal dealer, or if it is satisfied that the licensee does not carry on business at any of the sites identified in the licence, or that a site manager named in the licence does not act as site manager at any of the sites identified.

If a licensee or site manager is convicted of a relevant offence, the authority may vary the license by adding one or more of the conditions set out in Section 3 (8).

Any revocation or variation takes effect when no appeal is possible or when an appeal is finally determined or withdrawn.

CHAPTER SEVEN
BAN ON CASH

LASPO's ban on cash is re-enacted in section 12 of the Scrap Metal Dealers Act 2013, which provides:

"Offence of buying scrap metal for cash etc"

> *(1) A scrap metal dealer must not pay for scrap metal except-*
>
> *(a) by a cheque which under section BIA of the Bills of Exchange Act 1882 is non- transferable, or*
>
> *(b) by an electronic transfer of funds (authorised by credit or debit card **or otherwise**)."*

The Supplementary Home Office Guidance explains at paragraph 9.1: *"Only payment by a non transferable cheque or an electronic transfer will be acceptable. This will mean that the payment will be linked to a readily identifiable account, for both the payer and payee.*

The decision to ban cash appears to have been based on the assumption that the ban would result in the opening of bank accounts by suppliers (sellers) of scrap metal. Receipt of funds into identified bank accounts can be relatively easily traced, unlike cash and is likely to facilitate enforcement.

Crossed cheques

A crossed cheque is made out to an individual or company and may not be made payable by the payee to anybody else. It must be paid into the payee's bank account.

However cheque cashing companies may cash such cheques. Some of the larger metal recyclers have arranged for cheque cashing companies (cash converters) to provide their services from kiosks at the scrap metal yards. This means that the seller of the metal leaves the yard with cash in his pocket, as he did before 3 December 2012. Respondents to the Home Office review suggested that the provision of cheque cashing facilities at scrap metal sites be banned to reduce the risks of dealers circumventing the legislation.

The cheque cashing companies are subject to the Money Laundering Regulations 2007 and the "Know Your Customer" regime. They require proof of a name and address before cashing a cheque. The cheque is cashed. The cash is given to the payee who sold the scrap metal and the cheque is paid into the cheque cashing company's bank account.

Although the cheque cashing company keeps a record of the transaction and the name and address of the payee, it is more difficult to trace the payment by the scrap metal dealer through the cheque cashing company's account to cash in the hands of the payee, than it would be through the payee's own bank account.

The situation is further complicated by the fact that it is quite common for the supplier of the metal to ask the dealer to make the cheque payable to a third party: such as a mother, girlfriend or friend. When that cheque is cashed at a cash converter on the High Street it is difficult to prove that the supplier has received any financial benefit from the transaction.

Evidently, these situations were not anticipated when section 12 was drafted. No doubt it was for these sorts of reasons that some members of the metal recycling industry initially refused to install cash converters on their sites. They argued that they were not in the spirit of the law. However, despite the Home Office guidance, they are within the letter of the law and those organisations who were the first to appreciate this possibility and obtain good quality legal advice obtained a commercial advantage.

Electronic Transfers

The electronic transfer of funds may be authorised by credit or debit card *or otherwise.* This phrase is very broad in scope.

The Home Office Supplementary Guidance at paragraph 9.4 approves the use of:

> *Re-Loadable Electronic- Money products which are issued to a named account (which verifies the customer's identification) and undertakes full customer due diligence and "know your customer" checks under the Money Laundering Regulations ...Single non-reloadable pre-paid debit cards and re-loadable debit cards which are anonymous in nature and require only simplified due diligence under the Money Laundering Regulations are unacceptable.*

Anecdotal evidence indicates that some scrap metal dealers are using cards for payment that may not be issued to a named account, where the supplier may not have undergone full "know your customer" checks. They sell the card for, say £9.00, to the seller of the metal. They then load the card with the price of the metal. The seller uses the card to obtain cash from the nearest

ATM. These cards may be obtained over the internet simply by providing a name and address which is not verified.

However, any sort of payment by electronic transfer is likely to be lawful within the meaning of the Act. The Home Office guidance indicates that single non-reloadable pre-paid debit cards are unacceptable, when in fact they comply with the wording of the section. The breadth of the wording means that section 12 may not achieve its intended objective of ensuring that suppliers of scrap metal open bank accounts through which their business dealings can be traced.

CHAPTER EIGHT
IDENTIFICATION
REQUIREMENTS

The identification and recording requirements contained at sections 11 and 13 of the Scrap Metal Dealers Act 2013 came into force on 1 October 2013. The requirements may militate against adverse consequences arising from the breadth of the wording of the ban on cash, but section 11 gives rise to its own difficulties. For example, what are the requirements when making collections off site?

Section 11 provides:

Verification of supplier's identity

(1) *A scrap metal dealer must not receive scrap metal from a person without verifying the person's full name and address.*

(2) *That verification must be by reference to documents, data or other information obtained from a reliable and independent source.*

(3) *The Secretary of State may prescribe in regulations -*

    (a) *documents, data or other information which are sufficient for the purpose of subsection (2);*

    (b) *documents, data or other information which are not sufficient for that purpose.*

The Secretary of State has made regulations under section 11, setting out those documents that are sufficient proof of identity and address. The documents tend to be personal and held be individuals rather than organisations, with the possible exception of bank and utilities statements. The only document that does not require separate proof of address is the photo card driving license.

The regulations made under section 11 (3) may not be exclusive. In other words, the documents listed are sufficient to verify identity but they are not the only methods of verification that may comply with the requirements of the section. For example, a police warrant card is likely to satisfy the section and mobile collectors may not need to look at a person's photocard or passport every time they take a delivery on house to house calls. At present the police are accepting other methods of identification from mobile collectors, since it is impossible for collectors routinely to require sight of the documents listed in the regulations. However, the Home Office and local authorities take the view that the documents listed in the regulations are an exhaustive list.

It is also important to note that the section does not restrict verification methods to documentation. If a reliable and independent person were to provide spoken confirmation of the name and address of a supplier that might be sufficient, depending on the circumstances.

Section 13 Records: receipt of material

Section 11 (4) provides:

> *If the dealer receives the metal from a person, the dealer must keep a copy of any document which the dealer uses to verify the name or address of that person.*

The Home Office was initially prepared to consider giving guidance on how often identification documents should be physically checked and re copied. It has not published any guidance on this.

"Person"

This word is not defined in the Act. The Interpretation Act 1978 provides the following definition: *"Person" includes a body of persons corporate or unincorporated.* " In other words, a person can be an individual and also an organisation such as a partnership, or a limited or unlimited company.

The Secretary of State appears to have understood the word as referring to an individual when making regulations under section 11. He confirms that a photo-card driving license is sufficient proof of identity, as is a passport when combined with proof of address. Many scrap metal dealers are rightly checking the driving licenses of drivers making deliveries in order to comply with the section.

However, organisations may fall within the meaning of person and the regulations may not provide an exhaustive list. Furthermore, the heading of the section refers to the verification of the supplier's identity (arguably the person or organisation selling or providing the metal). This may be quite distinct from the driver of the load and many suppliers are organisations.

On a strict interpretation of the wording of the section, not only the driver but also the identity of the supplier may need to be checked, especially where they are not one and the same entity (where the driver is not an employee of the supplier for example). If it were otherwise the purpose of the Act, to prevent metal theft, might arguably be defeated. A suspect organisation might escape detection by arranging an appropriate driver for delivery. This is especially the case where the purchase price is not to be paid into an identifiable account, or is to be paid to someone else.

In practice, supplier organisations are generally routinely checked via their VAT registration.

"Receives"

This word is not defined in the Act. It has been used rather than "buys" and this means that a supplier cannot bypass the identification requirements by giving scrap to a dealer. It is likely to cover the physical handing over of the metal by a driver as the servant or agent of a supplier. It is also likely to cover the physical handing over of the metal off site, during a collection for example. Such a collection might be made via a subcontractor haulage company rather than the dealer.

Problems are caused by the absence of anybody to receive the metal from off site, such as when collecting skips. In that case it is not possible to check any person's identification and arguably checking the supplier will suffice. In other cases it is not practicable to ask the site foreman to produce his passport or driving license to prove his identity. On that scenario other methods of identification might conceivably be considered, such as telephoning the supplier.

The Home Office was initially prepared to give guidance on what the requirements meant when dealers were collecting scrap off site pursuant to a contract with an organisation. It considered that it would be sufficient to verify the organisation's identity. That guidance is not contained in the published version.

When considering licensing applications the police remain concerned to establish that identity checks are being made when scrap metal is collected by the holder of a site license off site, particularly where it is received from individuals with white vans.

"Verify"

This is the most important word in the section. The point is to verify, in other words confirm the accuracy of the name and address provided.

The identification requirements, although straight forward on their face, may not properly fit the reality of how the industry operates. There is no Home Office guidance.

CHAPTER NINE
DATA PROTECTION

In order to comply with the verification and recording requirements, scrap metal dealers are required to process personal data (information) about their customers. This processing is regulated by the General Data Protection Regulation (GDPR) and the Data Protection Act 2018 (DPA) ,and scrap metal dealers must be registered with the Information Commisioner's Office. The personal data is frequently contained in photocopies of driving licenses and bank account details. If this information were to be lost or stolen, there might be significant risks to data subjects of identity theft and other crimes.

In order to demonstrate compliance with the data protection legislation, and ensure that the rights to privacy of individuals are protected, it is advisable for scrap metal dealers implement data protection policies and appoint a data protection lead for their organisations. The lead is responsible for ensuring compliance with the policies, for providing staff training, for conducting audits, risk assessments and data protection impact assessments, and for dealing with data breaches. He or she also handles queries and complaints from data subjects about the processing of their data, including complaints from consultants and members of staff.

The data protection legislation requires scrap metal dealers to provide information to customers and staff explaining what is done with their personal data. This information is usually provided in a privacy notice that is accessible on the organisation's website.

Date controllers and data processors

Scrap metal dealers are data controllers. This means they decide why personal data needs to be collected and how to process it. Support providers, such as IT companies, are generally data processors. This means they have little discretion and must process personal data in accordance with the instructions of the scrap metal dealer. Under Article 28 of the GDPR there are specific clauses that must be included in contracts between data controllers and their data processors.

Meaning of personal data

Personal data are any information from which a living individual can be identified, either directly or indirectly. The information is not limited to names and identification numbers, or to photographs or addresses. For example, it may be a large shoe size, if there is an individual in an organisation known to have big feet. It also covers expressions of opinion about a person.

The personal information that scrap metal dealers process about customers and visitors to their yards is generally collected directly from the individual and limited to the following:

- Names

- Addresses

- Dates of birth

- Driving licenses and passport numbers

- Photographs, including CCTV footage

- Vehicle registration numbers

- Bank details and financial information

The staff information processed is usually:

- Names and contact details

- Dates of birth

- Financial information

- Health information

- Education, work history and qualifications

- National Insurance Numbers

- Next of kin and contact details

Health information is particularly confidential and falls into a special category of personal data. Any information revealing an individual's racial or ethnic origin, political opinions, religious or philosophical beliefs, or trade union membership, genetic and biometric data, health information and data in relation to a person's sex or sexual orientation falls into this special category. Scrap metal dealers have additional legal obligations in relation to that information.

Data processing

Processing covers any activity involving personal data such as collecting, receiving, sharing (both externally and internally), storing and destroying personal information. Information should be processed, only where strictly necessary and shared on a need to know basis.

Typically a scrap metal dealer may share customer personal data externally with:-

- Cash card companies

- Cheque cashing companies

- IT companies

- CCTV surveillance companies

- Accountants

- HMRC

Lawful bases for processing personal data

The processing of personal data is unlawful unless a legitimising condition, or lawful basis, applies. Scrap metal dealers may generally rely on the following legitimising conditions:-

- Section 11, Scrap Metal Dealers Act 2013 which requires the dealer to verify a customer's full name and address before buying metal;

- Section 13, Scrap Metal Dealers Act 2013 which requires the dealer to keep records of the documents used for verification, such as passports, utilities bills and driving licenses, together with the registration number of any vehicle that delivered the metal purchased.

The processing of contact details such as telephone numbers and email addresses is likely to be necessary to facilitate the smooth running of the business. It may be processed lawfully as it is in the business's legitimate interests to do so.

Information obtained through CCTV footage may also be lawfuly processed since it is in the dealer's legitimate business interests to keep the yard secure and prevent and detect crime. When assessing whether it is in the legitimate interests of the business to carry out surveillance, the scrap metal dealer should weigh up whether the rights to privacy of individuals outweigh its business interests in filming them. Generally, the balance is likely to fall in favour of the scrap metal dealer since there is a significant risk of crime within the industry.

Like other employers, scrap metal dealers process information about employees in order to give effect to their contracts of employment. For this reason it is likely to be lawful.

When processing special category data, such as health information belonging to its staff, scrap metal dealers must rely on an additional legitimising condition in order to process these data lawfully. A dealer generally relies on:

- Employment law obligations or

- Explicit consent.

It is important to ensure that any consent may be withdrawn as easily as it was given.

Data protection principles

Where there is a lawful basis for processing personal data, a scrap metal dealer must also make sure it carries out its personal data processing activities in accordance with the principles contained in the GDPR. They are:-

- lawfulness, fairness and transparency

- purpose limitation (processing solely for the purpose for which the data was collected)

- data minimisation (ensuring data is adequate, relevant and limited to what is necessary for its purpose)

- accuracy (ensuring data is accurate and, where necessary, kept up to date)

- storage limitation (ensuring personal data is retained for no longer than is necessary for its purpose)

- integrity and confidentiality (ensuring data is processed securely

Accountability

The GDPR requires organisations to ensure that data protection is embedded in the business at all levels of decision making and becomes fundamental to its culture. This is known as the accountability principle. Not only must a scrap metal dealer comply with the GDPR but it must be able to show it complies. Written polices demonstrate compliance, so long as it is clear they are implemented. It is advisable to have data protection, data security, data subject request and data breach policies in place. A privacy notice provides the required information to individuals about the personal information the scrap metal dealer processes about them.

Data protection impact assessments

Data protection impact assessments are a way of implementing the accountability principle. Whenever there is a significant change in processes or procedures, which entail a risk to data subjects, they ensure that data protection risks are evaluated and eradicated or reduced at the very earliest stage. Such impact assessments might be carried out where there is a substantial upgrade to an IT system, a new CCTV camera system is introduced or the system altered, or a new cloud provider is engaged.

Data protection impact assessments are generally carried out by the data protection lead.

Data minimisation

Data protection by default is as an aspect of the minimisation principle. In other words, no more data should be collected, shared and stored than is strictly necessary to achieve its purpose.

Retention periods

The retention periods for the personal data stored by scrap metal dealers should be set out in the data protection policy. Generally:-

- Documents used to verify identity are retained for three years in accordance with section 15, Scrap Metal Dealers Act 2013;

- Other personal data is retained for six years for accounting and auditing purposes

Security

Security is one of the most important requirements under the GDPR. Like other businesses, scrap metal dealers must take organisational, physical, and technical measures to ensure that their personal data are secure. Hard copy as well as electronic data should be processed in accordance with a documented security policy.

It is important that all members of staff comply with the security policy. It is advisable that failure to do so be a disciplinary offence that may result in dismissal.

Personal data breaches.

The data protection lead is responsible for responding to personal data breaches. He or she notifies the Information Commissioner within 72 hours where there is a risk to data subjects. The report contains a summary of the nature of the breach, the steps taken to reduce the risk to data subjects, and measures to prevent the breach from happening again. Where there is a high risk to data subjects, they too are notified. Reference should be made to the organisation's data breach policy.

Rights of data subjects

Data subjects have eight rights which include:

- Right to be informed about what the scrap metal dealer does with their personal data;

- Right of access to personal data by means of a subject access request;

- Right to rectification of inaccurate data, and to add to the information the organisation holds about the data subject if it is incomplete;

- Right to erasure, otherwise known as the right to be forgotten;

- Right to restrict or put a "block" on the processing of personal data

- Right to object to any processing carried out by the organisation based on its legitimate interest;

It is advisable for scrap metal dealers to have a data subject access request policy. The organisation must respond to requests from data subjects within one month.

Data protection risk register

All personal data processing activities should be recorded in a data protection risk register held by the data protection lead.

Personal data breaches should be recorded, whether they are reportable to the ICO or not.

The risk register should contain a copy of audits, risk assessments and data protection impact assessments.

Enforcement and disciplinary action

In many cases failure to comply with the GDPR and DPA is a criminal offence and can result in large fines. It is important that all staff are aware of the company's data protection polices, receive training in data protection, and that the policies are properly implemented.

It is advisable that any staff failure to comply with the data protection and associated policies be a disciplinary offence which may lead to disciplinary action and dismissal.

Privacy notices

Privacy notices should contain the following information:-

- Contact details for the data protection lead;

- A list of the data subject's rights to privacy under the GDPR;

- A description of the personal data processed, the reasons why it is processed and the legal basis for processing it. The legitimate interests of the scrap metal dealer should be identified where they are relied upon;

- Where reliance is based on consent, notification that this may be withdrawn at any time;

- The retention period for the personal data. How long is it kept for?

- The persons with whom the personal data is shared;

- The right to lodge a complaint with the ICO.

CHAPTER TEN
ENFORCEMENT

<u>Right to enter and inspect</u>

There is a right of entry and inspection of any licensed site under section 16 (1) *at any reasonable time on notice to the site manager* . The right may be exercised by a constable or an officer of a local authority.

There is a right of entry and inspection without notice where there have been reasonable attempts to provide notice and they have failed, or entry is required in order to ascertain whether the provisions of the 2013 Act are being complied with, or *for investigating offences under it and the giving of notice would defeat that purpose.*

There is no entitlement to use force.

Under section 16 (5), a justice of the peace may issue a warrant authorising entry to a licensed site premises or premises that are not licensed *if there are reasonable grounds for believing that the premises are being used by a scrap metal dealer in the course of business* (section 16 (6) (b)) and entry is reasonably required so as to secure compliance with the Act or ascertaining whether the Act is being complied with.

Under section 16 (7) the warrant is signed by a justice and specifies the premises concerned and authorises a constable or local authority officer to enter and inspect within one month from the date of the warrant. Reasonable force may be used if necessary.

Importantly, under section 16 (9) a constable or officer of a local authority can require production of and inspect any scrap metal kept at any licensed site premises, and at any premises that is subject to a warrant. They may also require production of and inspect any records kept in accordance with section 13 or 14 and any other records relating to payment for scrap metal. Copies of extracts from the records may be taken.

If the owner, occupier or other person in charge of the premises requires the officer to produce evidence of identity or evidence of his authority to exercise these powers he must do so under section 16 (11).

Closure orders

The police and the local authority have power to close a scrap metal yard where either is *satisfied* that the premises are being used by a scrap metal dealer in the course of business and the premises are not a licensed site (see paragraph 2, schedule 2 to the Act). There is no power where the premises are residential.

Contents of closure notice

The relevant provision is paragraph 2 (3), Schedule 2 of the Act.

The notice states that the constable or authority is satisfied that the premises are being used by a scrap metal dealer in the course of business and are not licensed for this use. The reasons why they are satisfied are provided .

A warning is given that an application may be made to the court for a closure order.

The steps which may be taken to ensure the premises are no longer being used by a scrap metal dealer in the course of business are set out.

Closure notice recipients

In order to begin the closure process the authority or the police must give a closure notice to the person who appears to be the site manager and any person who appears to be a *director, manager or other officer of the business in question*: paragraph 2 (4) Schedule 2 of the Act.

Where a person occupies another part of any building or structure of which the premises forms part , and the constable or local authority *reasonably believes* that person's access to the other part would be impeded if the closure order were made, that person must also be provided with the closure notice.

Cancellation of closure notice

Under paragraph 3 of Schedule 2, a notice may be cancelled by a cancellation notice issued by either the police or authority. It takes effect when it is given to *any one of* the persons to whom the closure notice was given. The cancellation notice must also be given to anyone else who received the closure notice.

The notice may also be provided to any person who is the owner, leaseholder or occupier of the premises although this is not obligatory.

Application for a closure order

So long as the premises are (still) being used by a scrap metal dealer in the course of business, or *there is a reasonable likelihood that the premises will be so used in the future,* either the police or authority may make a complaint to a Magistrates Court for a closure order, so long as this is done within not less than seven days of issuing a closure notice. The longstop deadline for making any application is six months from the date when the closure notice was given.

Where a complaint is made the justice of the peace may issue a summons directed to any person who received the closure notice, and which must be given to all persons who received the closure notice, to answer the complaint. The summons will set out the date, time and place at which the complaint will be heard. The procedure is in accordance with sections 51 to 57 of the Magistrates Court Act 1980.

Closure order

If the court is satisfied that paragraph 2 (4) has been complied with and that

(a) *the premises continue to be used by a scrap metal dealer in the course of business, or*

(b) *there is a reasonable likelihood that the premises will be so used in future*

as described at paragraph 5 (1), *the court may make such an order as it considers appropriate for the closure of the premises under paragraph 5 (2).*

Under paragraph 5 (3) the order may specifically require:-

- that the premises be closed immediately to the public and remain closed until the police or local authority certify under paragraph 6 that the closure order is no longer needed;

- that the use of the premises by a scrap metal dealer in the course of business cease immediately;

- that any defendant pays into court a sum determined by the court to be released when the other requirements of the order are met

The order may may such provision as *the court considers appropriate for dealing with the consequences if the order ceases to have effect as it is no longer needed under paragraph 6.*

Notice of closure order

The complainant must fix a copy of the closure order in a conspicuous position on the relevant premises as soon as practicable after it was made: paragraph 5 (6) of Schedule 2.

Cancellation certificate

Where a constable or local authority is satisfied that there is no longer any need for the closure order it *may make a certificate to that effect* under paragraph 6 of Schedule 2. The closure order ceases to have effect when the certificate is made and the court must release any sum paid into court to the defendant.

As soon as practicable after making the certificate, the police or local authority must provide a copy of the cancellation certificate to

- any person *against whom the closure order was made*: paragraph 6 (5) (a).

- the designated officer for the court which made the order: paragraph 6 (5) (b).

It must also *fix a copy of it in a conspicuous position on the premises in respect of which the order was made* :paragraph 6 (5) (c).

Application to court for discharge of closure order

A person who was given a closure notice and *any person with an interest in the premises but to whom the closure notice was not given* (paragraph 7 (1) (b)) may make a complaint to a justice of the peace for discharge of the closure order. The court may not discharge the order unless it is satisfied there is no longer a need for it: paragraph 7 (2).

Where such a complaint is made the justice may issue a summons directed to the police or local authority requiring that person to appear before the Magistrates Court to answer the complaint: paragraph 7 (3). All persons (other than the complainant) who received the closure notice must be provided with notice of the date, place and time when the complaint will be heard :paragraph 7 (4). The procedure is in accordance with the Magistrates Court Act 1980.

Appeals

Paragraph 8 of Schedule 1 concerns appeals.

An appeal may be made to the Crown Court against a closure order or a decision not to make a discharge order, by any person who received the relevant closure notice or any owner, leaseholder or occupier of the premises who was not given the closure notice.

The local authority or police may appeal to the Crown Court against a decision not to make a closure order or against a discharge order.

Any appeal must be made within 21 days beginning on the day when the decision was made.

The Crown Court may *make such order as it considers appropriate.*

Enforcement of closure order

It is an offence to fail to comply with a closure order *without reasonable excuse*: paragraph 9 (1) (a).

A constable or *authorised person* ie a person authorised for these purposes by the local authority *may (if necessary, using reasonable force) enter the premises at any reasonable time and, having entered the premises do anything reasonably necessary to secure compliance with the order:* paragraph 9 (2) (a) and (b). This is a broad and sweeping power.

If the owner, occupier or other person in charge of the premises requires evidence of the officer's identity or evidence of the officer's authority to exercise those powers the officer must produce it: paragraph 9 (4).

It is an offence to obstruct a constable or authorised person in the exercise of these powers:(paragraph 9 (5).

CHAPTER ELEVEN
CRIMINAL OFFENCES

<u>Carrying on business as a scrap metal dealer without a licence</u>

A person who carries on business as a scrap metal dealer without a licence commits an offence under section 1 of the Act punishable by an unlimited level 5 fine. This offence is committed by the scrap metal dealer, be it an organisation or an individual, and its directors or officers.

<u>Other offences punishable with Level 5 fines *(unlimited)*</u>

Failing to comply with section 12 and the requirement to pay for scrap metal by cheque or electronic transfer is an offence punishable by a level 5 fine, as is any failure to keep records of the receipt and disposal of scrap metal as required by sections 13 and 14, including a copy of the cheque used to make payment or the receipt identifying any electronic transfer. Where there is no receipt, the dealer must record particulars identifying the electronic transfer. Furthermore, the person making the payment on behalf of the scrap metal dealer must be identified on the record.

These offences may be committed by the scrap metal dealer, the site manager and the person who made the record. There is no defence for the person who made the record but the site manager and dealer will escape a conviction if they can prove they made arrangements to ensure compliance with the section and took all reasonable steps to ensure those arrangements were complied with.

Where a closure order has been made, it is an offence to permit premises to be open in contravention of the order or to contravene the terms of the closure order in any way: (section 9). It is also an offence to intentionally obstruct a constable or authorised person when exercising his powers of entry (if necessary by using reasonable force). Both offences are punishable by Level 5 unlimited fines.

Offences punishable by fines at Level 3 on the standard scale (£1,000)

These offences include failing to notify the local authority of material changes, making a false statement in connection with a licence application, failing to display the licence, failing to verify the supplier's identity, obstructing a right of entry or inspection and failing to produce any records kept in relation to the receipt and disposal of scrap metal. The same defence is available for the dealer and site manager as set out above.

Offences by bodies corporate

Under section 17:-

(1) *Where an offence under this Act is committed by a body corporate and is proved –*

(a) *to have been committed with the consent or connivance of a director, manager, secretary or other similar officer, or*

(b) *to be attributable to any neglect on the part of such individual, the individual as well as the body corporate is guilty of an offence and is liable to be proceeded against and punished accordingly.*

(2) *Where the affairs of a body corporate are managed by its members, subsection (1) applies in relation to the acts and omissions of a member in connection with that management as if the member were a director of a body corporate.*

Where an individual or corporation has been convicted of a criminal offence in the Magistrates Court, the prosecution may apply for transfer of the case to the Crown Court in order to obtain a confiscation order in relation to the proceeds of the crime.

CHAPTER TWELVE
CONCLUSION

The wording of the Act is broader than appears on an initial reading and appears to be broader than intended. There may be individuals and organisations trading in scrap metal that do not know they are caught by the Act.

The test of "suitability" is undefined and unlimited and has encouraged some Authorities to consider making stipulations of their own when deciding licensing applications, which appear to be outside the parameters of the Act.

The breadth of the wording of section 12 means that suppliers of scrap metal continue to leave yards with cash in their pockets and without a bank account, although it seems that traceability through bank accounts is what was initially envisaged when the Act was passed. Furthermore, there is no bar to making payments to third parties. The ban on cash is perhaps not as effective as it might have been.

The identification requirements are deceptively simple. They have triggered wholesale checks on drivers, and left dealers wondering whom to check when they themselves are in the driving seat when collecting off site.

As part of his review of the Act in 2017, the Home Secretary was required to consider the objectives intended to be achieved by the Act, whether those objectives had been achieved, and to *assess whether it is appropriate to retain or repeal the Act or any of its provisions in order to achieve those objectives*: section 18 (2) (b). He consulted with interested parties, seeking their views on whether the Act had contributed to reductions in metal theft. Many respondents complained about the need for the legislation to be more effectively and consistently enforced. The Home Secretary noted that enforcement was outside the scope of the review which was focussed on the effectiveness of the Act itself.

The report makes reference to metal theft offences recorded by the police which showed *a continuing downward trend in numbers of offences* during the five years to the end of March 2017. It suggests that 30% of the reduction was achieved by (1) Operation Tornado in 2012 (a police initiative which required scrap metal dealers to request identification documentation for every cash transaction and retain copies for twelve months); (2) cashless trading which commenced in December 2012 with the introduction of LASPO and (3) the Scrap Metal Dealers Act 2013 which came into force on 1 October 2013.

In response to a number of suggestions on how the existing legislation could be strengthened, the Home Office confirmed that it would give consideration to this in future, in consultation with interested parties and taking into account the representations received in response to the review. In the meantime, there remain concerns that local authorities and the police may lack the financial resources to enforce its provisions, which could put those organisations who comply at a commercial disadvantage.

The Act may generate case law, before too much longer.

MORE BOOKS BY
LAW BRIEF PUBLISHING

A selection of our other titles available now:-

'Ellis on Credit Hire – Sixth Edition' by Aidan Ellis & Tim Kevan
'Tackling Disclosure in the Criminal Courts – A Practitioner's Guide' by Narita Bahra QC & Don Ramble
'A Practical Guide to TOLATA Claims' by Greg Williams
'Artificial Intelligence – The Practical Legal Issues' by John Buyers
'A Practical Guide to Prison Injury Claims' by Malcolm Johnson
'A Practical Guide to Hackney Carriage Licensing in London' by Stuart Jessop
'A Practical Guide to Advising Clients at the Police Station' by Colin Stephen McKeown-Beaumont
'A Practical Guide to Antisocial Behaviour Injunctions' by Iain Wightwick
'Practical Mediation: A Guide for Mediators, Advocates, Advisers, Lawyers, and Students in Civil, Commercial, Business, Property, Workplace, and Employment Cases' by Jonathan Dingle with John Sephton
'Planning Obligations Demystified: A Practical Guide to Planning Obligations and Section 106 Agreements' by Bob Mc Geady & Meyric Lewis
'A Practical Guide to Crofting Law' by Brian Inkster
'A Practical Guide to Spousal Maintenance' by Liz Cowell
'A Practical Guide to the Law of Domain Names and Cybersquatting' by Andrew Clemson
'A Practical Guide to the Law of Gender Pay Gap Reporting' by Harini Iyengar
'A Practical Guide to the Rights of Grandparents in Children Proceedings' by Stuart Barlow
'NHS Whistleblowing and the Law' by Joseph England
'Employment Law and the Gig Economy' by Nigel Mackay & Annie Powell
'A Practical Guide to the General Data Protection Regulation (GDPR)' by Keith Markham

'A Practical Guide to Noise Induced Hearing Loss (NIHL) Claims'
by Andrew Mckie, Ian Skeate, Gareth McAloon

'An Introduction to Beauty Negligence Claims – A Practical Guide for the Personal Injury Practitioner' by Greg Almond

'Intercompany Agreements for Transfer Pricing Compliance' by Paul Sutton

'Zen and the Art of Mediation' by Martin Plowman

'A Practical Guide to the SRA Principles, Individual and Law Firm Codes of Conduct 2019 – What Every Law Firm Needs to Know' by Paul Bennett

'A Practical Guide to Licensing Law for Commercial Property Lawyers' by Niall McCann & Richard Williams

'A Practical Guide to Adoption for Family Lawyers' by Graham Pegg

'Essential Motor Finance Law for the Busy Practitioner' by Richard Humphreys

'A Practical Guide to Industrial Disease Claims' by Andrew Mckie & Ian Skeate

'A Practical Guide to the Law of Armed Conflict' by Jo Morris & Libby Anderson

'A Practical Guide to Redundancy' by Philip Hyland

'A Practical Guide to Vicarious Liability' by Mariel Irvine

'A Practical Guide to Claims Arising from Delays in Diagnosing Cancer' by Bella Webb

'A Practical Guide to Applications for Landlord's Consent and Variation of Leases' by Mark Shelton

'A Practical Guide to Relief from Sanctions Post-Mitchell and Denton' by Peter Causton

'Butler's Equine Tax Planning: 2nd Edition' by Julie Butler

'A Practical Guide to Equity Release for Advisors' by Paul Sams

'A Practical Guide to Unlawful Eviction and Harassment' by Stephanie Lovegrove

'A Practical Guide to the Law Relating to Food' by Ian Thomas

'A Practical Guide to the Ending of Assured Shorthold Tenancies' by Elizabeth Dwomoh

'A Practical Guide to Financial Services Claims' by Chris Hegarty

'The Law of Houses in Multiple Occupation: A Practical Guide to HMO Proceedings' by Julian Hunt

'A Practical Guide to Unlawful Eviction and Harassment' by Stephanie Lovegrove

'RTA Allegations of Fraud in a Post-Jackson Era: The Handbook – 2nd Edition' by Andrew Mckie
'RTA Personal Injury Claims: A Practical Guide Post-Jackson' by Andrew Mckie
'On Experts: CPR35 for Lawyers and Experts' by David Boyle
'An Introduction to Personal Injury Law' by David Boyle
'A Practical Guide to Claims Arising From Accidents Abroad and Travel Claims' by Andrew Mckie & Ian Skeate
'A Practical Guide to Chronic Pain Claims' by Pankaj Madan
'A Practical Guide to Claims Arising from Fatal Accidents' by James Patience
'A Practical Approach to Clinical Negligence Post-Jackson' by Geoffrey Simpson-Scott
'Employers' Liability Claims: A Practical Guide Post-Jackson' by Andrew Mckie
'A Practical Guide to Subtle Brain Injury Claims' by Pankaj Madan
'A Practical Guide to Costs in Personal Injury Cases' by Matthew Hoe
'The No Nonsense Solicitors' Practice: A Guide To Running Your Firm' by Bettina Brueggemann
'The Queen's Counsel Lawyer's Omnibus: 20 Years of Cartoons from The Times 1993-2013' by Alex Steuart Williams

These books and more are available to order online direct from the publisher at www.lawbriefpublishing.com, where you can also read free sample chapters. For any queries, contact us on 0844 587 2383 or mail@lawbriefpublishing.com.

Our books are also usually in stock at www.amazon.co.uk with free next day delivery for Prime members, and at good legal bookshops such as Wildy & Sons.

We are regularly launching new books in our series of practical day-to-day practitioners' guides. Visit our website and join our free newsletter to be kept informed and to receive special offers, free chapters, etc.

You can also follow us on Twitter at www.twitter.com/lawbriefpub.

www.ingramcontent.com/pod-product-compliance
Lightning Source LLC
Chambersburg PA
CBHW061612220326
41598CB00024BC/3561